Henry Ford and the Car

Nicolas Brasch

Contents

Cars, Cars, Cars......................................3

Who Was Henry Ford? 4

An Expensive Luxury 6

Marvelous Mass Production..................8

Cheaper Cars 10

The Moving Assembly Line.................12

A Changed World...............................14

Glossary...16

Cars, Cars, Cars

Only 100 years ago, there were more horse-drawn carriages than cars. Cars were far too expensive for most people to buy. Today, however, many people can afford cars. There are more than 500 million cars in the world today. That number grows by the millions each year! How did this happen? To find out, we need to look at a man named Henry Ford.

Most people used horse-drawn carriages in the early 1900s.

Who Was Henry Ford?

Henry Ford was born in 1863. Henry loved playing with machines when he was a boy. When Henry was 12 years old, he saw his first engine-powered **vehicle**. From then on, his mind was rarely on school. He thought about engines instead.

Ford left home when he was just 16 years old. He headed to Detroit, Michigan. There he found work in a **machine shop**. He was an **apprentice**, or junior worker. He fixed engines. This was the start of a working life that would make Ford one of the most important people of the twentieth century.

Henry Ford was interested in engines from a young age.

Henry Ford, standing on the left,
spent his early life working with engines.

An Expensive Luxury

By the early 1900s, there were many carmaking companies in Europe and the United States. Some were very small. However, some grew into large companies that are still making cars today. One of these companies is the Ford Motor Company. It was formed by Henry Ford in 1903.

The first car Henry Ford built looked like a box on wheels.

In those days, people **manufactured**, or made, cars one at a time. Because they were made one at a time, cars were expensive. However, Ford had other ideas. Ford wanted everyone to be able to buy a car.

In the early 1900s, only rich people could afford cars.

Marvelous Mass Production

Henry Ford decided that he had to do two things to make a cheaper car. First, he had to build just one **model**, or type, of car. Second, he had to **mass produce** the car. This meant making thousands of cars at the same time in exactly the same way.

Ford named his car the "Model T." He sold the first one in 1908. The Model T was tough, reliable, and affordable. It cost less than half as much as cars from other companies. Americans loved the Model T. More than 10,000 Model T's were sold in the first year.

Many Americans swapped their horse-drawn carriages for Model T's.

THE PARK COMMISSIONERS
HEREBY FORBID ANY ONE FROM
DEPOSITING ANY FILTH, OR RUBBISH
ON THIS BEACH,
UNDER PENALTY OF LAW.

A WRITTEN APPLICATION WILL BE
REQUIRED BY THE PARK COMMISSIONERS
TO ENABLE ANY PERSONS TO ERECT, OR
MAINTAIN ANY BATH HOUSE, OR
OTHER STRUCTURE ON
THIS BEACH.

Cheaper Cars

By 1926, a Model T cost just $290. How did Ford get the cost so low? Ford looked at every single task that had to be completed to build a car. He then figured out the fastest way to do it. The result was the **moving assembly line**.

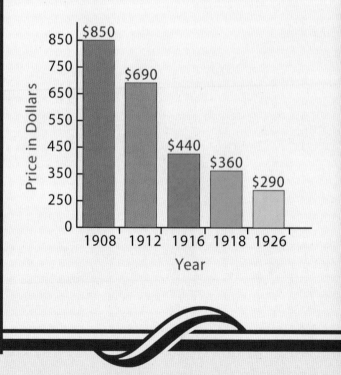

Price of a Model T

The moving assembly line changed factory work forever. Ford's workers stood in one place. The cars came to them. Each worker had just one task, whether it was to put in a bolt or tighten a screw. The moving assembly line made building cars faster and cheaper.

Ford's workers stayed in one place while the cars moved up the assembly line.

The Moving Assembly Line

The assembly line was simple and quick. The Ford factory could make one car every 24 seconds. Each Model T coming off the assembly line was the same as the one made before it and the one made after it.

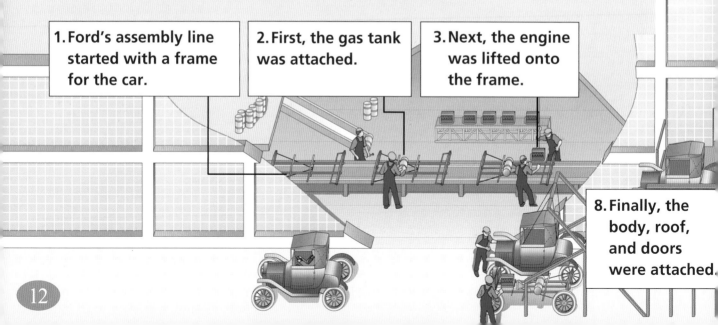

1. Ford's assembly line started with a frame for the car.

2. First, the gas tank was attached.

3. Next, the engine was lifted onto the frame.

8. Finally, the body, roof, and doors were attached.

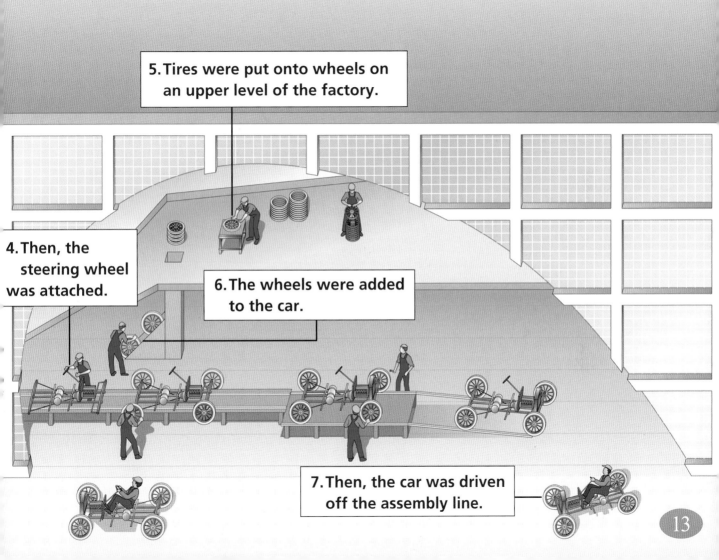

5. Tires were put onto wheels on an upper level of the factory.

4. Then, the steering wheel was attached.

6. The wheels were added to the car.

7. Then, the car was driven off the assembly line.

13

A Changed World

Robots have replaced people on car assembly lines.

Henry Ford died in 1947 at the age of 83. He did not invent the car, but his ideas about cars and manufacturing changed the world. He wanted cars to be affordable for working people, not just the rich.

The moving assembly line made owning a car possible for most people. Car factories, as well as factories that make other products, still use the moving assembly line. Ford's ideas and how he put them to use changed the world and the way we live.

Today, many people around the world can afford to own a car.

Glossary

apprentice a person who learns a trade or skill

machine shop a place where metals are cut and shaped

manufacture to make or produce goods

mass produce to make a large number of the same thing

model a specific type or design of a product, such as a car

moving assembly line a line of workers or machines along which a product is moved as it is made

vehicle something used for carrying people or things, such as a car